confusion matrix
and
other poems

confusion matrix
and
other poems

david j. murray

iUniverse, Inc.
New York Lincoln Shanghai

confusion matrix and other poems

Copyright © 2007 by David James Murray

All rights reserved. No part of this book may be used or reproduced by any means, graphic, electronic, or mechanical, including photocopying, recording, taping or by any information storage retrieval system without the written permission of the publisher except in the case of brief quotations embodied in critical articles and reviews.

iUniverse books may be ordered through booksellers or by contacting:

iUniverse
2021 Pine Lake Road, Suite 100
Lincoln, NE 68512
www.iuniverse.com
1-800-Authors (1-800-288-4677)

Because of the dynamic nature of the Internet, any Web addresses or links contained in this book may have changed since publication and may no longer be valid.

The views expressed in this work are solely those of the author and do not necessarily reflect the views of the publisher, and the publisher hereby disclaims any responsibility for them.

ISBN: 978-0-595-45577-5 (pbk)
ISBN: 978-0-595-69586-7 (cloth)
ISBN: 978-0-595-89878-7 (ebk)

Printed in the United States of America

Contents

Introduction ix
Confusion Matrix 1
I 66
    Derivation 66
    Sublimation 67
    Reconciliation 68
    Decoration 69
II 70
    On hearing Bach played on a great organ 70
    On seeing the score of the last song of Schubert's *Winterreise* 71
    On hearing Richard Bradshaw's *Ring Cycle* 72
    Das Rheingold 72
    Die Walküre 73
    Siegfried 74
    Götterdämmerung 75
    In memoriam S. George Laverty, MD 76
III 77
    On the fear of going mad 77
    Paranoia 78
    Hospital 79
    Madmen then 80

    The madman now 82

IV 83

    Sacrifice 83

    Oblivion? 85

    Brooding 86

    Dove in death 87

    Death-in-life 88

    18th-century death 89

    Thinking 90

    The atheist's death 92

    Purgatory 95

    Stealth 96

    Standing and watching 97

    Gravestones 98

    Vistas 99

    Wordiness 100

    Quiet light 101

    Casket 102

    Retrospect 103

    Why? 104

    Fear 105

V 106

    Child awakens 106

    Child at play I 107

    Child at play II 108

    Child at play III 109

    Child at night 110

    Child asleep 111

VI 112

    The nerves 112

    The veins 113

    The storm 114

    Alone 115

VII 116

    Night-thought 116

    Illicit love 118

    Epithalamion 119

    Museum piece 120

    Truth 121

    Knight 122

    Desire Poem 123

    Form 124

    O thou 125

    Theme 126

    Variation I 127

    Variation II 128

    Variation III 129

    Variation IV 130

    I do not like you, but I … 131

    I do not like you, but … 133

    I do not like you … 135

    I do not like … 136

    I do not like this … 137

    … but *they* do 138

VIII 139

    Seasons 139

Spring I 141

Spring II 142

Autumn 143

Dawn 144

Morning 145

Daytime 146

Nighttime 147

IX 148

Still Life by Cézanne 148

Departure from Cythera by Lorrain 149

A Chair by Van Gogh 150

A Soldier by Rembrandt 151

A Girl On A Swing by Fragonard 152

Work by Holman Hunt 153

Water Lilies by Monet 154

Dancing Girls by Matisse 155

An Op Art painting by Vasarely 156

X 157

Rainbow 157

Rhetoric 158

Inspiration I 159

Inspiration II 160

Invocation 161

White goddess 162

In the mists 163

INTRODUCTION

A 'confusion matrix' refers to a printed table showing how often a person listening, say, to the telephone confuses the sound of one letter with that of another. For example, the sound of 'M' might be confused with the sound of 'N'. In testing how well a new telephone system is operating, a technician might ask a number of participants to listen to a sequence of letters spoken over the phone and write down, after each, what letter they thought they had heard. A table can then be constructed showing how often the sound of 'M' was confused with the sound of 'A', 'B' and so on up to 'Z'. The table will show, for example, that the sound of 'M' is confused more often with the sound of 'N' than it is with the sound of 'K'.

The subtitle of *Confusion Matrix* is given at the start of the eponymous poem as *A Pavane for the Death of Certainty*. Just as the word 'waltz' can refer either to the dance itself, or to the music written for a waltz to be danced to, so the word 'pavane' can refer either to a dance that was popular in Renaissance Europe, or to the music for that dance. Usually, a pavane was a slow dance for several couples, but it has also had a specialized meaning, namely, a slow dance performed by a single performer at a solemn commemoration of the recent death of a member of a royal family.

The following verses, therefore, depict, in a dance-like rhythm, the sense of sadness that accompanies the loss, by a person, of certainty about something. What that 'something' is will vary from person to person. Confusion is here viewed as a feeling in its own right that can cause strong emotions no matter what the confusion is about.

Following the long poem *Confusion Matrix* are several sets of short poems; these sets were not originally written as such, but were put together for the purposes of this compilation from files containing poems written at different times over many years. But no matter what the topic, there is a common undercurrent that matches the feeling-tone of *Confusion Matrix*. For example, the last five poems in the set about romance demonstrate a confusion in the writer's mind about the desirability of being attracted to somebody he does not really like very much. However, most of these poems are stand-alone works that do not necessarily have to be considered within the context of the set that includes them.

I wish to express my deep gratitude to Sylvia Hains, PhD, and to Rachel Breau, MLIS, for their assistance with the preparation of the manuscript for publication; and to Esther Murray, née Mongrain, for her patience and encouragement during the writing and processing for publication of this not-so-slim volume.

Confusion Matrix
A Pavane for the Death of Certainty

1

Into the hollow of this heightened care
I wove my way because I did not dare
To desecrate the name I did not bear
Nor don a uniform I dare not wear.

Nothing but earth exists, and out of earth
Is born the squalor of your birth
And all the looks they say you're worth:
Your height, your ankle-depth, your girth.

Nothing but earth doth constitute
The link 'twixt earage and lute,
The carnage of a clay Beirut,
The shine of an old and damaged suit,

The mellifluities of wine,
The cackled call of 'Auld Lang Syne',
The madnesses of the benign,
The dust within the flowing Rhine,

The architecture of a spire,
The grandiose burning of a lyre,
The nothingnesses of a choir,
Lost as darknesses draw nigher.

All is earth, there's nothing more:
Earth in foibles, earth in store,
Earth in pastness gone before,
Earth beneath the hearthwood floor,

Earth as I look at the dark'ning night,
Earth where starriness seems blight
Against the blackness's delight,
In being of earth and born of fright.

2

When everything is dark and forest-dull
And into Earth's noisiness falls a lull
That heralds the quick fingers of the pull
Of silence filling what was never full,

Then does that silence grow like leaves
On the ancient tree that Man believes
Is shelter for a Density that weaves
Destinies for which no goddess grieves

Nor which the whiles do restlessly inspire
Storymen, tellers of lies that fire
Their listeners to think there is a higher
Person, to even greater falseness to aspire.

Into this silent space that earth contains
Fall, as from gods, relentless rains
That breed, on the drooping conifers, refrains
Of drops and splats till life regains

Its readmitted, rudimented song
That nothing has been changing all along.
Only the weather rights its wreakèd wrong,
And only the earth stays stiff or weak or strong.

Nothing can move a mountain up to stand
And stalk in precipices o'er the land,
Cragging its ruts with rocks and sand,
Seeking its hilly hollows to expand.

Nor can an anteater on water move
Feetlets and nostrils in aerial groove

Not a drop wet the better to prove
That even on earth, water can love.

Nor can a thunder blast so loud
That terrestrial monuments be cowed
To shatter and fall in a dusty cloud
That even the lightning can enshroud.

3

And into this golden haze of nothingness
Nary a finger is stretched to bless
The unwoven shrapnel of a leopardess
Or the unteazel'd tinsel of a tress;

And into the darkening days of the Night
That spreads its reticence recondite
Over the veiled and valleyed height
Of a plateau enforested, bold and bright,

In the lazy appalledness of the Sun,
Stretching its crazy hands like One
Over the tentacled Amazon,
Splitting its lights, centurion.

Into those lightening nights do spread
The thousand encounters of men with dread
And the forest, like hairs couturèd,
Stands tingle-green in the glows of the red.

Darkness prevails and the only sound
Is volcanic murmurings underground
While twitter-a-tweet in the forest around
Stealthily silences; murder is crowned;

Darkness aflames th'unpenetrated world:
Elegance slinks, her flags are unfurled,
Medium moderates, vagueness is hurled
As if challenge to newborns still curled

Sleek and asleep in mother's smooth lap.
Arms and legs closer around her enwrap.

Oh! That this baby-hope please overlap
The death-wish encompassed within every nap

Taken in secret on embosomed life
Of working and waiting and bosomy strife
That lingers 'twixt birth and the cut of the knife
That severeth body of Senex from wife

And isolates him into starting again
A body from birth unto death in new pain,
Slowly a-sagging yet taut in that rain,
Washing the corpuscles free from his brain,

Downpour on downpour, lashed in the rain
With the bittersweet absence of absolute pain,
Just a warm comforter, bleeding again
With the wanted and wanton legerdemain

Of nothingness folded, arm, leg and hand
In the smooth and warm holding, nothing unbanned,
Warm in the wet and weak humanoid land
Of whimper that babies can all understand.

The cycle from flesh unto flesh, born and dead,
Alkali-acid from toe into head,
Umbilic-torn, penis askew, new-furrowèd
The hairy cave of the wed and unwed.

Black is the darkness of the forest lanes,
Chronic the call of the forest's refrains,
Blatant the weakness as victory drains
From the floor of the forest into the plains

While mountains mock, edgèd in stony rock,
Upon the wide circumference of the bloc

Where strive the strivers and the fleeing flock
Huddle, minion'd, ruled by the clock,

And wait for brazen reuniting, bare,
With the silent skin of Awaiting where,
Fealtied with flesh, angels bear,
On shards of smoothened lust, her hair

As if it dealt, merchantman-like,
With Something out there it was not like;
Something out there it did want to like;
Something out there it really could not like.

4

One looks in vain and barren hopelessness
For an encounter-countering redress,
For an improvement left to make the mess
Less clear and less redundant, always less.

But chaos is a mindful thing; what lives
Knows nothing of how mathematics gives
To ordered reigns of sinews, veins, reprieves
From being predictable and forgives

All desecrations of the legal line
Marking the edge of what is 'mine' from 'thine',
And crossing the crux from anodyne
Pure 'chance' unto the dangers of 'divine'.

Neither does a thing that creeps and crawls
Across the sun-dried stretch between two walls
Know that its armoured tentacle appals
The armoured knight who from his palfrey falls.

Nor does the knight whose fear doth seem to touch
The armoured vault of Heaven, for so does such
A blue-on-sun-dried sky appear as much
As an emptiness, dare to besmirch

The near-perfection of the randomness
With human adroitness or befoul the 'less'
With 'more', or wade wild rivers in undress,
Letting his armoury clank with loneliness.

His head hits the ground, gross, unhelmeted
Where the heart-stopping scuttler fled

From this wall unto that while blood unshed
Stops the knight's brain from being unshacklèd.

Flee into darkness, thought, bridlèd be,
That pure entrancèd moments can spring free
Back in the bed where baby-you and she
Knew what was felt could purge the irony

Of knowing the seen was the sure and safest way
To aggrandize the minimal and replay
The softest touch of silkiness all day,
All day, until the daying light gave way

To darkness and goneness murdering pure thought
And elongating night to purest nought—
A long-spun thread of nothingnesses brought
To a point where nothingness is sought.

No need to chide a Super-Consciousness
Where one quick blade of *sensu* can impress
On passive languor lost in listlessness,
The urgent imperfection of excess.

And the trenchant lines that mark the thighs
Of the world thou meetest in thine exercise
Seem to encounter skeins of skin that rise
Full and a-networked, premise of demise

Upon that lone and blissful innered place
That you would feign determine is your space
In this wide world where there is no disgrace
In filling thought with feelings that replace

All propositions of a probable kind
With sidewind sensibilities that find

Hunger associated with the keenest mind
Latches apart and sense is unconfined.

Back, back to the sky where what a fledgling sees
Is the same as the growèd crow, and seize
The snapshot of the furrowed forest trees
Caping the shining rivers' tentacles

Of shining ribbons shot in craze of green
Where none of the morbid things are seen
That crawl beneath the rivers' glossy sheen
And live as if thought, and life, had never been.

5

With all the clarity of bright-eyed truth
Bards make amenities of their youth
And, glistening, glide to serve their trade uncouth
The whiles a-muttering beneath their breath

That the clean cascade of the cleansing waterfall
Is making murk and griminess of all
The green and non-affronting overhaul
They hoped to make of what is slime or caul

And, in each and every caterwauled cliché,
They solemnly and oh so humbly pray
That the dirt they shake from the prayers they say
Will away and cleanse their prophecies for aye.

But dirt and smoothness work their magic power
And cause the filigree of every flower
To make amends for the slowness of each power
When nothing works to further their amour

And, glistening, gliding, the rhymesters move
To massacre each lust with words like 'love'
All in a heat the while to try and prove
Their oneness is intact with One Above

While the poor slimy slimesters listening abed
Slither to prove their ecstasies unwed
Are something of whose snakeskin powers unshed
That meld in will with what the poets said

And a benign father, apeface all agrin,
Stares from the highest tree over the forest's green

And tries to shake, from thoughts of being seen
As powerful, his fears of being too thin

And worthy therefore of a saint's demise,
So eagerly does he dream and dramatise
His joining of the skins and agonize
That were he blinded, still he would have eyes,

While over and across the greener-eyèd roof
Of the forest as attested from his loft aloof
Slowly a colour darkens, of Anger Nature's proof,
A slow incarnate tension of a Thunder's wrath

Breaking the skies with slots of sullen red
And batteries of bright lightnings overhead
While, completely sheltered in their floory bed,
Slimesters and grinners alike wriggle instead

Of stopping to cleanse their frenzied minds of gore,
Of palimpsestic anarchy of more
Or yearnings to finish the What had gone before:
This slickened tension riddled every pore

With longing for completion—brains can plan!
The notion of a Logos makes a Man!
Hiding within its huddled skinsters can
Contempt for meditation slowly span

The circumscribing outer face that waits
For plans to fall till enterprise abates
And nothing but purest wanting advocates
The falling into dust of all debates,

All lust to sit on high, over the trees,
All designated archery to please

Other a-seated entrailed dignities
Watching aloft for spontaneities

That filter into words all that is felt,
But stumble, for no feelings are misspelt
Or gelignite-like ignited into words like *Welt*
That characterize the planned and not the felt,

That auger-like deplanes the affrighted lines
Into something more miniscule than Valentines
Or something more majestied that combines
Love for the Royal with passionate designs.

6

The wincing leer of manifested mind
Restrains the proffered offers of its kind
And consecrates to Mammon what its blind
Untested oracles deliver undefined;

Even a solid vein of calcined rock
Standing upsided, sediment of rock,
Can in a windwash of upended rock
Stiffen and fall a-crash on new-fall rock,

Thus scaring up stark memories of screes,
Scrabbled bedebris lacking any trees,
And footfalls loud and scraped upon the breeze,
And libertine frolics in those memories

That must bedashèd be in molten mind,
Lending its philosophies unrefined
To stiff and starken bolstered humankind
Running away from what its searchings find,

The attractive leadership of age
That, free of work, is once more free to gauge
Approximations of its present wantonage
To the olden days of freedom in its cage

Of simple flesh, colour be damned,
Tactifically manifest, telegrammed
In smoothness, monogrammed
In letters decorous and warmed

By constant contact with the warmth and sheen
Of she whose skin and contact must have been

Warm and literate, smooth and velveteen,
A glorious pre-literature of the skin.

Age, as it streams so slowly to the now,
Burdens its bearers with reminders how
Babyness was unburdened and the brow
Of growth and adolescence was enow

Bedighted with all burdens and all sorrows
To cast onto its brow its rustic furrows
Some a-riven by Cupid's many arrows
And some derived from indignation's bows;

Age steals a solemn plot from Nature's play:
Each day we age brings on another day
Wherein we, stricken, beg our leave to pray
Return, redemption, to our mother's splay

Of arm on little arm, hand in holden hand,
Chest on bulging breast, talk blessedly banned,
Thought pleasantly blocked, wants pleasantly bland,
The happiest little lazy-bones in all the land,

Till Age grows back and we the future feel
Where bones are rare to knit and wounds to heal
And the enconjuring joints scarcely anneal
What strains had stretched what fluids to congeal;

Clothèd against the furtherings of the clime
That pits the fiercest weather against time
And causes rage against the skies to fume
And ecstasy to forge a sky sublime:

Housèd against the chatterings of the snow,
Roofèd to keep the heat in here below,

Heated to keep our skin in clothèd glow,
Only a glumming outlooking can grow

When the minds of the social softly blow
And outlook we do onto art or TV show
Or gaze at the garden's red rustiness or stow
Into our fictional middle all the flow

Of fictions out there that stock the artist's store
And carry our charabanc heads into more
Of the clean and away from the shore
When the sea waves' washes and forests restore

And where the barking dogs assail the moon
To enter once again her time at noon
When in the dark of fertile Hallowe'en
All things were living in perceptual swoon

With not a jot or tittle of adventureness
But all perceptual onenesses were less
Than a blessèd continuity of blissedness
Bordered and ruffed by wantlessness

Except for perpetuation of the present 'this',
Unbroken save for the odd occasional kiss,
When breath breathes out until, unremiss,
Tactile injection restores the lovely 'this'.

And back into non-freedom sinks the mind,
And back into All-feeling Humankind
The momentary godness falls behind
And thought becomes once more quite undesigned,

Excrescence of a budding neuron's fear
That something from the Outer crouches near

And stands to threaten what is bright and clear:
The Now, the 'this', with modulations drear

Of a 'what if?' or 'whither?', questionettes
That skither like alcoholic epaulettes
On the smooth shoulders of refresherettes
Blathering bleakly of serviettes,

All a bewildered dream of what might be
That 'tards and emblemishes what you see
While feeling falls and the 'thises' flee
And only dark 'whys?' rive my 'me' from 'thee'.

Back to the dark we surge to flee
Where moons are high noons and mystery,
And, unto the utter edge of what we see,
All that is nothing appears to be

A something that is cause for inner dread,
A pirated peak rearing its icy head
Over the lower rifts of reveried
Mistiness, purged and unpowerèd,

Flat in the silk of pure talk and thought:
Worries unwanted, worries unsought;
A ball of pure glass in a window-light caught;
A puff of bright knowledge that nobody taught.

Such temptings to break the gloss of the 'this',
Such envies to tense and to snap, unremiss,
This golden moment of golden bliss,
By thinkings of 'that' and of 'that', not of 'this'.

Broken the graven cord that crossed the span
Linking mother to babe and woman to man;

Broken the difference 'twixt noontime and sun,
The mountains of mourndom are overshone

By colours that hail from the flake of the day,
Chasing the shadows of Laughter away,
Encouraging murmuring thoughts of display,
Ploughing the air into disarray

Where once was Night, and Moon and Noon
Were One and the Sun was a one-time None,
All linked together in sensory swoon
With arrogant Shame easy to shun.

And liveried limes were thingdoms-to-be,
A wasting of sense into poetry,
A grieving of Being, a garbage of Glee,
A poison outspread of a thought-life unfree

To trammel, quick and efficient, a symmetry
Of sensing and thinking to one melody;
Only discordance resonates free,
For freedom of feeling is assonance-free.

7

Oneness in one's life dare no religious preach:
They are the murderous breaths of evil's outward reach
And act as the opposèd side of what they teach
And serve as cannon firings that morality breach.

Oneness has no place for an outer god;
He or she is a mental composite, an odd
Amalgamation of a father's rod
And a mother's laugh at what her man is not.

Oneness, when flared in fullest consciousness
Makes all the rest seem coloured emptiness;
Hence the imposèd dream of Art's redress
For the confusion of social multi-ness.

The fullest is so full that nothing more
Can penetrate that moment's tidal bore,
That wave of washing oneness that bears o'er
All smaller thoughts its flush veneer,

Making the small the smaller and the great
The lesser, 'arrogant' to 'abrogate',
'Multiplex' to 'sole', 'delayed' to 'late',
And love of rest to wakened wanton hate.

That which affrights one's lust for purest Thee,
Neighbour, real, human, giving unto me
Onenesses unlimited, parched to be
Twonesses entrapped in non-eternity

Of moments breaking, with unmighty zeal,
The truth of Nighthood with the stainèd Real,

The love of the one with the darkened Sociale,
And Pleasurèd Goodness with wordy Appeal,

All vicious encounters with Vultures of Steel,
Redolent raptors, ready to feel
With Talons of Talent the bowels that unreel
And the bones on which blood-gouts await to congeal

And the starkorèd bones that new sunsets reveal
And the wastes of endeavour where nunneries kneel
To plead that the lawgivers never repeal
The law that says: Thou shalt not touch the Veil.

Thou shalt not touch Thyself. Thou shalt not touch.
Touch thou shalt not. The feelings are too much.
They threaten out that murderers and such
Are lesser Lovers than are those who touch

The Veil and thereby shake, *too* much,
The wander'd ways that lead to Perfect Touch,
That lead to execrations of the much-
Malignèd arts that consecrate the Touch

To enlivened Goddesses, artifacts of mind,
Muses, Gaias, Feminines refined
To gallery goddesses, sometimes being kind,
Lifting a thigh or showing a behind,

Or sometimes cruel, mobbing the mad
As punishment for thinkings *going* bad,
But all the while sheer artifacts, to be had
For a song or a sonnet or a sad ballade.

They lift, however, with their sad refrains,
The long between-times, the pouring rains,

From wait-time into sunlight that regains,
For unfleeting moments, the regal strains

Of the music that signals Oneness comes near:
The dearth of the Whole makes that music more dear.
The music will last till the klaxon cries 'Here
Is Endeavour requited! I signal, All Clear!'

And Oneness comes, Sopor undoubted, free
As the thought-link that binds me to Thee.
And all the endeavours of Philosophy
Melt to a Nothing, a truly Dead Sea.

8

Trust my resource of loudly sounds but not their appeal
To your goodness, for never in that case will ever avail
The strength of the sensuous waiting to steal
From your golden accoutrements ecstatic, a wail

That will shudder across the darkening mountaintops,
Waking the sleepers, extorting Calliopes
Into their own interlashings of never-stops,
Beast unto beast, breast into breast, tops

Unto bottoms, enticing the rivulet's course,
Staying the way the night bestraddles its horse,
Blatantly stating in emerald words the source
Of the sounds, the loudly sounds, resource

From the depths of which cometh each line that I write,
Straddling horses that straddle the night,
Flagrant in metaphors stainèd with light,
Endless harassment of endless delight.

Resource—oh!—soft ego, for Thee claim I me
And watch all the wandering women with glee,
Knowing 'tis I that should go on my knee
To suckle them brazen were I not so free

In my freedom of oneness with eloquent she
Whose movements portray all her oneness with he
Who, like a stupid dragon grins in his mockery
Of this, poetic cloud, symbol of minstrelsy,

Failure of simple attempting to be
Struck by—oh!—sticks or similar stimuli

Lifted aloud to cuckuck-land, free
To spout, eggily, wondrously, hopelessly

Of failure, failure, failure in words
That strike the land like God-droppèd shards
That evocate death like black-wingèd birds
That scream for a gigolo's sharp-sheathèd swords.

9

I see my life as fervent vales and squanders
Where what is not fixed in bed endlessly wanders
Through quid pro quos as Inner-Ich re-ponders
Why answers never come to corresponders

Who question me with endless kindly gazes
Firm and fix that endlessly amazes
The Inner-Ich that endlessly re-raises
The Outer as surprises turn to crazes

And a simple look a-shake across a room
Scatters what mordant remnants of a tomb
Lies in memorial silence in the gloom,
Echoing its fidelity to the womb

The Outer first made *connaissance* before
The Inner that its inner silence bore,
Hummèd and pampered, metaphor
Of all the clinic agonies in store

For an unborn Soul whose inner chemistry
Laughed at atoms in a mockery
Of genic phallacies and of camaraderie
Atwixt the sexes in the life-to-be,

Burdening life with a brainchild born to be
Thinker insolvent, parched debauchee,
Battling battles with stammered repartee,
Buying with nothing, nothing one could see,

Frivolous waste, a spender of good cheer,
Waster of *luxe*, waterer of beer,

Blind in both lobes, worse than a seer
With Nordic halterments and stifled leer,

Worse because blindness brings out what is clear
In each of the storms that threaten every year
Of life, till the death of Christmas makes appear
That one small Gift can fill an atmosphere.

10

O Eyes that gaze from mountaintops of Mind,
How can you seek, and, willing it not, re-find
The ghastly gauntlet that the mentally blind
Must run is not restricted to your kind?

O do not chide me from the wondrous deep
Of those your signet eyes that sentry keep
O'er the part-entries that can never sleep
But only, dormant, wink at what they reap.

Do not belabour me for wanting Thee
As symbol of the one who wanted me
And hung, as if from a sword-hung velvet tree,
Her hopes upon my brain-work's anarchy;

I'm a poor being, moving, feet-ground, through air
That fills the space between the owlen stare
Of thee, ensconcèd in thine envious chair,
And me, walking to no one knows where;

I have myself been cheated, playing fair,
And wandered blankly down a hotel's stair
And watched the stars scud across a sky of vair,
Furrèd with clouds that don't go anywhere;

When mental minds in-penetrate like locking
Arms that drag a laggard to a shocking
Height, where shuddering veers to blocking
And minds beat vainly as on blank doors knocking

Till nothing is but what is mentosphere,
Word inchoate that no one wants to hear,

Word to beat down as arrogance made sheer,
Word that will not in any book appear;

Till then thy body shall have formal skin,
Thy hair shall wrap thy sculpted head within,
Thy clothes will sing like sensual songs of sin,
And all thou art shalt sing Thee champion.

11

Were Love and Hate to linger by this brook
And lean into the wind to write this book,
Fretting a finger forward in order not to look
At viciouser zephyrs men mistook

For looks upon a pussy-fated past
And almost blew, at footstanders aghast,
A flame that wrenched the sail from off the mast
And blew it in the sea, iconoclast,

With white for love and living-rippèd hate
Both in uncolour, pallid reprobate,
Incarnate food, refreshing in the late
September of a three-scored apostate

Life shrunk to death, inertia borne away,
Watching the crassness drift from day to day,
Undoing what was done as acrid play,
Denizens work with scars of disarray

And poisons what light would be were light not sour
With missing accomplices waiting on an hour
When all with a fullness would be filled, and power,
That throbbed each vein as if it were a flower

With fullness to be filled, with rain up-stem
And colour unfold in Nature's stratagem
To pin new vestments to the rainbow's hem
And turn each tinselled raindrop to a gem,

Were indeed love and hate ever to shake hands
Or bow unstinted in unloosèd sarabandes

Or, saddled, ride cross-kimbo over sands
That blew like dust nets over holy lands,

And boundaries unholy that did brook
No curious questioning why a book
That fillèd was with 'do not, do not look'
Should hang my heart upon a steely hook.

12

And is the dark betrayal of your whole
By your mind an indication that your soul
Phantasm is that emptinesses stole
From your mind in order that you scroll

The past upon a screen thrust on your mind
To make you to your emptinesses blind
And scatter over all your thoughts unkind
Blandnesses so that you will never find

The emptinesses lurking in your dreams
Where wholeness but an acrobatic seems,
Twisting stark remnants of events to reams
Of paper'd pictures of your life's extremes;

And never see the blatant truth of smiles
And never know concoctioned ready wiles
Or the heart that slivered eyingness beguiles
Or the Oh! that 'twixt-two-people reconciles

And never beyond the veildom penetrate
Until the door slams shut and, profligate,
You expurgate your innocence too late
And let your whole on moralnesses wait

And never see what sights outwave the blue
That shimmers over the harboured wavelets' hue,
Glisten and crystal, bob and thread anew,
Tinselling all the water-swelling through;

And never hear the soft white voice of dawn
'Tice the entrancèd dew unto the lawn

And cock-like bring the dam unto the fawn,
Scattering whispers poet-mocks to spawn;

And senseless fall in nothingness bereft
Of what the mind had of your wholeness left
Spurning even a touch, a laugh, a cleft,
Daftness in daftness rendered super-daft

Existence, in a mass of earthy green
That a dress can cause of plenitudes unseen
Standing arrayed before a flower-decked screen,
Bringer of beaker'd wholeness so obscene

That words do fly like shockeries serene,
Trying to scrub the Universe more clean
But failing, failing: who has always been
The purest is the dirtiest at the scene.

The cleanest is a bearer of address
Phallopic, skimming with elegant finesse
The purest planes of skin, *délicatesse*,
Unfinished, born of politesse,

A subtle slide of close-together flesh
Meeting that two intwinnèd minds enmesh,
Wholeness adroit from sudden eye-coins rash
That tar the toney sky with honey'd brush

And a slow weep, on details concentrate:
A pore, a wisp, as details aggregate;
A flake, a nail, a lock emancipate
From surface, digit, hair anticipate

Of the hollow whole that soon will cry of nought,
Of total ecstatics from vague thinking brought,

Of a negritude incipient from a bought
Offering to the beings that we ought

To be, gods, but which we cannot be
Because all gods have only cruelty
To flagrantly announce their cold divinity:
Mercy is weakness and mortality.

So we go search, through endless walls of time,
What we can capture within a human rhyme
Of what, through blood, is an orrery sublime
Of non-encounters that come close to crime.

13

If I too poor and uninspirèd be
More to enact than scorn on mockery,
What do these venal walls, these veils of glee
Shatter about and shard their spites on me?

Only the poor and cold and tired at night
Know what it is to shake their fist at light
And in their upside-downness congregate
To flicker dreams, like sperms, upon their spite;

For they were born as well as you and me
And know through an eyebrow-touch the congeries
Of the hold upon their hold that lets them see
The horrid boredom of the well-to-be;

And, staring through the tenemented snow,
Watching the snowflakes blow back to-and-fro,
Feeling the silence as if it were a glow,
They fiddle their feet with not a place to go;

Thus distillate their being on the air;
The air is warm *because* they do not care
That nothing, they all think, can e'er repair
The fatalizèd fact that they are there.

O booming bellow of a torrent-tide to be,
Scorn not thy handiworks that were not made by thee
But think, as the snow belabours lake and sea,
Of all that is nothing is stronger than needs be

And makes perfection into arduous renown
Where nothing funnier is than the clown

Who shortens life into his pudding-shapèd gown
And runs through drifting puddles through the town

Crying 'I made it!' as his sodden way
He makes from night to dusk and day,
Backwards a-foddering till his way
Is blocked by a tall and wide array

Of bricks and blocks all neat and stacked a-high,
Straining to scrape, with elevator-shafts, the sky
And call the electric daylight down to ply
Its trades upon the streets when they run dry;

And our clown with glossy-eyèd mien
Stares at the dryness of the scene
And wishes to stain it with obscene
Gestures that tell where he has never been.

There in the dawning light do dements die;
There in the snowmusk lies a fainting I;
There as the moon in rustic fledges high;
There where the wingèd seagulls swoop and cry;

There where the aging rusting of the fort
Annihilated is by fortuned Inns of Court;
And there is a diff-er-ence 'twixt 'I abort'
And 'I have missed' that can pertain to sport

But more to frantic graspings re the hold
That holds the blissful baby to the bold
And smoothened love of Mama's gold
As silver in her arms she doth unfold

And hold as tender armour 'gainst the fight
That folds her tentacles into her, tight,

While Titans wage their conflict *ohne* spite
Around her while the day turns into night.

She can alleviate, she, these brains
That spit their silences so none complains
Except the she who, as in trains,
Gazes to see the world slip by in chains

Born of unfreedom e'er to slip and dream
Of escapologies nurtured on a scream
And a wimping ladling from the stream
That ne'er produces butter from its cream.

14

When the dark cataract of lights
That spells the stars that spark the nights
That spill out ancient words and rites
Treaties 'twixt Earth and troglodytes

Falls and cascades across the black
That heaves like Heaven o'er the back
Of the Atlantid Atlas's back,
Bent in a supplicating wrack,

Human and want in simian pose:
Here is a hemlock! Here is a rose!
Then is the cataract He-Who-Knows
And its fine landfall adipose

With felony skin and feeling fine:
Half of a human, half divine.
Stretch it a little, heed its line;
Let it arraign, let it recline.

But always await that the waterfall
Jittered with stars can never appall
With idiot bleatings but only fall
Cascádent, episode-rental, till all

The stark skies of this Nighttime soul
Belly the earth until it's whole
And scratch out its universal goal
On the hinge of the universal Bowl,

Upturned and unwanting whatever the dawn
Shall hurl at its veils 'of thinnest lawn'

To spatter their melodies' magic and spawn
Tears 'stead of Turbulences born

Out of the cataract, out of the morn
That baby-like steps with steps forlorn
From Atlas's head, dazed like Anacreon,
Knowing not what of his sides he is on.

15

He who refuses to chant is still alive:
You cannot lock him; Nature makes him strive.
His will is further-reaching and can thrive
On minutes of new daylight that deprive

The cornucopic neurons of his brain
Of the black sustenance of thinking e'er again
Of e'er again of e'er again of e'er again
Chopping new genitures with that refrain,

As e'er again comes round in waves of rain
Flattening to turmeric the grain
That ne'er had grown had e'er again not grown
And ne'er can grow if e'er again

Be promulgate progenitor of refrain.
Oh do not think anew—oh!—ne'er again
Refrain from out-repeating e'er again
Till Sophocles doth mount a boy again.

And the dark waves of sultry cultures lash
The avoidable stretches of the sultry Wash;
Nay, cold is the Wash with lividific rash
Of sunset-sore on the widening gash

That the sun, untrammelled, has attained
In the watery gravel wet-attained,
In glorious freedom unrestrained,
Yearning for sunsets unconstrained

By pollute-retreats and genuflections,
Free of repeats and retrospections,

Free to just be in all-day reflections
Of rising and falling and choosing ejections.

Oh welcome, O Sun, that washes away
The epiparalysis of everyday;
Ever again, e'er again need to pray
For ever-enduring stillness sans play;

And when the will fails and the statics stand
Solemnly silent over the land,
Running the wheelings of birds by the sand
And ensuring that weaklings are banned from the band

Of robbers and tyrants and bellicose louts
Who hear not the whispers the North Wind shouts
Of woe to the weakling who Nature's law flouts
While giddy in glassness the wallflower pouts;

And anxiously on stare the ones who survive,
Younglings at anchor, ready to thrive
As the mists fall down on those who strive
To keep the natural laws alive

By bullying brilliance, bothering brain,
Watching the law work again and again
In the darkness beneath the downcoming rain
And its stench of psychological pain;

Anxiously on do they stare as the years
Filter by with their powers in arrears,
For the weaklings who cannot untune their ears
From the foldings and flailings of all their fears

The power-ones who call on the verily strong
To fight for the Natural Law when it's wrong

And unholiness clutters the watch-stretch long
Of the faith that has faded to nothing but song,

Nothing but music to chidden the night
Where the fears become fully absorbed into fright
And panic enchains the breast of the Right
And beats out the war drums of Wrong to fight

The elevation of wisdom to Height
Of Unknowing and Non-erudite
While in cells enhermitic glows a light
That cannot last long; it is not bright.

16

A breath of song-begetting sex
Sputters the light to sing and flecks
The sultan's private tower with specks
Of arrogant hope; the light bedecks

The silver town with convoluted rays
Yellow and burned to symbolize days
When the sun licked its hand to erase
Scalderings where light met blaze;

The light reveals in golden skeins
Where the tart forests greeted the rains
And the shuddering clefts of dark moraines
Spilled out their potions over domains;

The light attracts attracted lights
Of stars of frozen frosty nights
And warms the crystalline stalactites
Of icicle-stars to the hoary heights.

Light is the all that covers the sound,
Keeping it moaning down and around
The soiled architecture of the ground,
Trying to make it more profound.

The battering-rams of muted drums
Thump in near silences; Nature hums
Lyrical proxies for thunder-bums
Joviate, arrogant noisy-comes

That crisscross the lace of the countryside
And fetter in waxen ropes the wide

Spanses of water and waves to hide
Its joyous enjoyment of regicide;

Oh speak to it not: only use song.
Jiffy the parasites along
Who burdenate would, rejoicing with wrong,
With Joyce a cold voice lost in the throng,

Sing out the song to awaken the dead
And kill the amorphous-in-the-head
Who know not of poems they never read
Although they would feel them alone in bed;

This coruscate cataract of bliss
Sanctifies landscapes as crowded as this
Turning green mountains to histories
Written by lunatics who never kiss;

Oh crowd this subtle landscape full
With the bedlam of laproom and skull
And engine-lack lapping of push and of pull
And even extremes seem to nullen the dull;

Measure thy windward head, oh peak,
Brushing the sky with thy skullcap sleek
And gathering up thy forests to check
None have eloped or been otherwise weak;

Check its dark hairs, its whistling pines
And eloquent spruces and shuddering vines
That make as of play on the sloped inclines
A music driven by tropeic designs

Volts of apparel, ohmings sartorial
Cladding the cleats of the forest boreal,

Filling the branchèd spaces arborial
With sounds that make music memorial

Of what the forest-cries once heard,
As if a nonentity of a bird
Had acted the part of a creature furred,
Cheeping a growl from a glottis absurd

And wandering wakeless stirrèd the dark
With musical muscles before the lark
Escaped into upperdom there to mark
Its emptiness with a jolted spark.

17

There is no hiding-place can spell
The end of what the Fortunes can foretell
Nor can an evening repel
The dusty myth that men and women fell

From a state engraced to servitude
Under a state of Nothingness imbued
With a lack of moral turpitude
And a name that stomped the stuff from 'attitude';

No rock or cleft or cliff or gorge
Can foster certainty or treaties forge
That make the men and women merge
To a sheet wherein the ragged holes converge.

Mind is a poking out-hole stick
That moves across the whitened air so quick,
That filigree is mocked as 'sick'
And arabesques are thought of as a trick.

Oh leave that fevered hold of 'Now'
And come to where new steeliness can vow
Success, although the roadways plough
New tracks across a newly treacherous snow;

Then will mark-million's ochre hand
Be hold as conqueror o'er the waiting land
And feel his new-found standard stand
Firm while the wrigglers, dumb, disband;

And orreries turn and days unclasp
And minions mental lose their mental grasp

On musical makings of the harp,
Tending the stringed tendrils down to warp

And, beaten and clearly overlaid,
Ascribe their weary musings to a renegade
Who flaunted flowerings everglade
Bleating beneath their forest's balustrade;

Then are the weak more ardent than the strong;
'Tis they who spin their lives out into song
And decorate mere sonnets until long
Disheartened ballads fall disintegrate

Into stanzaic stanzas that prolong
Those who are weary of the right and wrong,
Wanting instead pure fairness to prolong
The long infinity of 'fitting in' song,

Turning harassment into new finesse
Echoing nakedness with undress
And finding the more to envelop the less
And adding new smells to *délicatesse*.

Away from the wondering world of the mind!
Follow the follies and greeten mankind!
Turn from the trystings! Pretend to be blind!
Let all your verses be written unsigned!

And in the recovery days near your death
Retrieve not the parchments of your breath
And mustiness-papers you thought were a wealth
That stole on your onslaughts with pestilent stealth;

But cling to the cringing one that you see
Carved on a park-bench, held in a tree,

Holding up Heaven on one hand to be
The other hand's craves in the blossomy sea;

And let the milky powder peter out
Like sand that has lost its potential to shout
And golden the waves that are lost on the shore
But palsies, collapses as shoals reef about

The innerway waterway lost in a surge
Of revisited violence ready to purge
The glorious night of the day in its mist
And die, blossomless, blameless, unminimalist.

18

How rooted in one Time are all our days!
Each is a centre filtered from the rays
Of rising and drowning suns whose every phase
Is set in the Dimension it displays;

A feeling's mirror matches what the sun
Is thinking when its day is downward done
And the rancour that has riddled it has run
Its course from climax to its *resolución*.

Two looks there are, the sun's, and that of me,
And all abjure the adolescent's spree
And wanting what is abstract and is free:
Only when feelings grow can he feel Thee.

And when Thou'rt lost behind his reverie
Only your cinematic motions can he see:
You are an artwork, hair-work floating free;
You are the one that he would want to be;

You are his goal where brain and mind agree
That what is unfelt can never, never be
Bespoke as fashion where an ancestry
Unkempt can form a sculptor's monody;

In lingering Laocoönic mastery
Flimsy the flowing stone falls silently
Over the hip and under the knee:
Only the stone exists; who cannot see

The fear that snaken coils evoke in Thee
Is born a turbulent Power-puff, to be

Doomed to enladen space with tragic history
And writings that entomb its melody,

Fit to repeat in words the rivalry
Between the dream and the open tyranny,
The dream of fusion and the slavery
Of thou and you diluted to a Thee.

19

All passion borrowed rarely can abate;
All fantasising lasts till Time runs late
And even for a fused reality a wait
Of more than days can rarely compensate;

All the entrenched adulteries of Art,
The Guineveres and Helens of the heart
Whose mindless bodies have no corporal part
Still spin the centuries out till Time restart.

Ancient and modern crown the literate days
Where to her Tristan crown-Isolde plays
Unceasing roles of model roundelays
And rounds unending that no dawn allays;

But all is sconced in a fine and mental frame;
Time takes no toll nor Work no idol fame;
Pure in the mind, no treachery seems tame;
There in the Real 'tis Honour takes all blame

For the *un*accepting, the fearing of being 'free'
To roundelay with she and thee and Thee
While anxious conscience windeth 'o'er the lea'
And pinnacles unconscious tower above the sea.

'Tis literal world of Stretch from sea to sea
Where figures toil and nowhere-places be
And sputtering villains push in empathy
With maidens who know not what else to be;

And spoilèd is what, numerate, Beauty yields;
Her shards of spite are spattered o'er the fields;

Incompetence cakes the pates of crownèd heads
And nothing crowns the cores of plays unreeled;

For Art is nothing but a feeling fine
That skirts the birth of Death and doth design
An ancestry that leads to serpentine
Pretensions that all paint is turpentine;

All music is forced silence and is never free
To complicate, as words do, ecstasy
But simply shows, unravelling, what we
As human cell-assemblies think we see

Of the passing world to a stop-clock symphony,
Each tock a passing clockwork-bee,
Each poisèd pause a whitened potpourri
Of mighty Nothingness's symmetry;

Each tock a picture tinct with black and white
Showing smooth nightshades growing in the night
And arrogant clouds shearing across the bright
And faceless moon that haunts the light;

Each tock is a Nell who, laughing, shows her thighs
To be *Lumpen*-right for those who like their size
While nymphlets, laughing eke-wise loud, surprise
The passing traveller with the love-light in their eyes;

And colour and sound now fuse the passing show
The silences seem coloured and, shadowy, to glow
As if anticipating how the pictures go
From mythic to a high Poetic low

Where anything I dream I also feel
Like You! Oh! My long-lost Wanderer!

Three times I felt my body-parts reveal
In Thee, as well, all that I could feel!

Where anything I dream I also feel
As things that carve their archwork to conceal
The fact that missèd moments never heal
But, in the soul, coagulate, congeal

Like dark pneumonias of the inner mind
That promise one will never, never find
Repeatment of those moments unrefined
Whose Truth met Cause in Copy undesigned.

20

Worry is only what the conscious says
To dignify dilapidated days
Crossèd with censure and dismays
That Nature Nothing now displays.

Thee is a conscious choice of evergreen
That filleth out the landscape and the scene
Making of future hills what they had been
Back at the time when freedom seemed obscene;

And when huge swathes of living cedars bore
Down from the clefts to the uncleft shore
Shrapnel of green that for ever more
Would serve as glasslight's living store:

Symbols of seeing while unseen;
Symbols of more than just a green;
Symbols of indolence epicene
And fears of a loss of what never had been.

Oh, you are not one of us; you are blind
To the simplest feelings of mankind.
All that you know is a chart so designed
That never your you-ness you'll ever find;

And reason sings clear with dominant eye;
Sheetings of blue sheet a competent sky;
All is clear-cluster and no-one but I
(I mean you) can elucidate why;

Why is there Nothing that links you and me
Save the knowledge that were I to say 'This tree

Is me' sheer blankness would dominate Thee
And awayness would sharpen a 'two' to a 'three'.

Such hyphens to clutter an uncluttered page!
Unity grovels to makeshifting age
While nothing has order to soften one's rage
And everything verges, trivial, persiflage.

21

And even a knight is no longer borne in
On carriage of gold as paladin
To be a bright ember conquering sin
When conquest of guilt is the best way to win

And easily mastered by having no thought
To entrap and to hold what one has brought
To one's parlour in pallor, the captivate caught
On a tether she wanted, a tether she sought;

But soon sought a tether, the freer to be
In non-thinkingness, mock jamboree
Of the thoughtless unbothered to feel or to see
The infinite boredom of what has to be,

Nature on Rockdom, the soft on the hard,
The free-flowing wetness, the hoisted petard,
The lime on the locksmith, the involute card
Of the pedant displaying before the retard;

And into this achronic anti-freeze
For relegating thought to expertise
Of lazing days and murmured symmetries,
That pith a kind of peace from reveries,

Into this pours a delectation for a past
That not existed once and may be classed
As humble-pie for dreamers of a vast
And dreamy Emptiness outpassed

Only by sorrowing grunts of grief and groan
That tell the dreamer he is on his own

Or she no longer has an 'own' to moan;
Only a Loss bestirs the grand Oblivion.

And coloured words and sonic paintings loom
Like doorways standing frontwards at a tomb
That sliddies backwards into deeper doom
While childish hands pick poems from its gloom.

22

All that is writ is wrote and spitted out;
It gouges like a writhing waterspout
Across the graves a-scattered all about
The grounds that graving History carved out;

When every corpse that ever lay dead still
Till putrefaction took its wanton will
And vanishèd the body into soil
That slowly into deeper ground would spill

Letting excessive hollows mull the earth
Into torpidic rollings hardly worth
The toil of mowing then is there no death
Of nothingness to mark that being's birth;

But writing there is on blessed marker-stone;
Writing there is the corpse can call its own;
Writing there is that solemnly can crown
A pile of soil with value and renown;

And music can be notated, written down
To fill a centuries-later morn with sound
And even the clashing seasons and impound
Their threatening beatings to confound

The dreary fuss of noises non-harmonic
With marvellousnesses vast and sonic
Singing a forest's velleities daemonic,
The forest-floor agorged with pandemonic

Sounds that flutter, groaning, passing by
En route to a greater greeting in the sky

While thunderstorms form a booming threnody
For this End of intellectuality

In Art and in Song and in all that Is:
Threnodies are the mists of histories
That bloomed afresh with better melodies
To bleach the darkness from our ancestries.

23

In the cool swell of the dark warm doors of death
Smells one the counting pulse-beats of Genesareth
Where 'twixt the waving palms the zephyrific breath
Of coolness of the glorious pools of nothing saith:

'Ohé, ohé', though I try to heave with light
All I achieve is a crescence in the night
And though I try, with words like 'grief' and 'blight'
To darken the world, I only make it bright.

I am the abandoned flailer, etching in 'monodies'
Achievement's flops, iatrogenic remedies
That make the canker worse and make new parodies
From serious utterings and jokes from threnodies.

As I passed my glorious hymnals along the rows
Of pettifogging jockerels and crows
I see how the muffled laughter hics and grows
And tipples the roofbeams with its furbelows;

For only in quietness is the songling mute,
A tender sort of carapace about his throat,
His twitching wings furling the air to float
Rapidwise to where the angels gloat;

Only in silent *Sprechgesang* downplayed
To glottal trivialities dismayed
And murder's beauteous hatred underplayed
And a listless lap with nothing up-displayed;

And only the silencing patter of the rain
Drops to uphold the voice's ochre pain

And colourless retrieval of its old refrain
That happy times come for the strong again;

And the listless tears of bardic plenitude
Turn on the tumbrils of their pulchritude
And show no signs of moral turpitude
So sunk they are, so stagnant is their blood.

24

And so ensconced in sameness's rude caves
They are that difference is a signature that saves
The poet from the death-in-blood he weaves
With his wastrel words that honesty deceives

And spurns a glorious starlit eye to a dull
Encounter with a looking-glass unfull
Of anything that could exert a useful pull
On the looker's wistful vista-full

Of herself. Oh bad, oh bad, seducer-boy!
Ne'er shalt Thou savour Her of Troy
In dream or writing or in bedded joy
Unless thou dost no metaphors employ

But only write Truth, a camera'd list
Of her glories and jollities ne'er unmissed
By the hands that engineer their tryst
With her, and hers with his, exoticist

Of panoramies stapled on a map of Greece
Like moths appallèd by the feel of peace,
Stuck in a lattice of no release,
A lyric of losses that never cease;

Or butterflies stuck on a gloss of Rome
Asking why Heaven should ever be Home
When the heart is not there, preferring to roam
Clumsily through earthsticks to find home

And pestering the Muses to let them attain
Verse to solidify pleasure and pain

On a vast trap-board to try to regain
A world of affectionateness once again;

And the paranoid stance of the baby's mind
No longer exists as he tries to find
Pleasure so strong he is momentwise blind
And only in books is discomfort defined.

25

A savage force of wanting never lends
Pretensions of robustness but portends
A slow leak of insanity that amends
The criminal inkling that intends

Simply to take, with whispers of no guile
What was a person satisfied to smile
Unblocking 'neath all Weight, and pile
Injustices upon them all the while

Deferring to a Will that has Its say,
That What-is-What can ne'er betray
The What-had-Been, but goes away
When What-will-Be comes into play,

And turn that person into hemisphere,
Half-world apportioned to appear
Good when a goodness hovers near
And dark when Darkness howls "All's clear";

A world-in-half that fades when *proper* fear,
Unsocial, unchaotic, hovers near,
Waiting for joists to jive and heave and jeer
As the house of hope collapses crystal-clear

Down on that person born beneath the Weight
Of broken maps and arcane surrogate
Bequests of being too soon and yet too late
For solemn questing's sense to dissipate.

How visibly trite are words when Might is Right!
Yet, by a hair, 'tis possible to fight

With pennant moments arch and recondite
That seem to paint new colours onto night

And take, with transformation's attitude,
Flowers that were lank and make them nearly lewd,
Hiding the stamen's strictures, seeing them imbued
With inks that were in Heaven's cloisters brewed,

And tinctured colours forged from Heaven's dyes
Causing the wilting flowerlets to rise
Like tiny choirboys trying to praise the skies
While jocularly pointing to their thighs

And standing firm with unsurprised surprise
As the flowerlets shudder further as they rise
And seem to ensprinkle starlets on the skies
As up they shudder, firm in colloquies

Of eloquence where words are feelings felt,
Moods affixed to paper e'er they melt,
Sentences improper properly a-spelt
And screams improper mitigate all guilt.

Words can spell properness; Law can spell 'right';
Words can spill blood; fear can spill fight;
Fantasies' flood can cool the hottest night
And barricade a being from his fright;

No worthy cause can dullen dewy Day;
A moment's thanks makes hollow causes gay;
Impostering makes floralets for May
And pattered sunshine-spots that fade away;

Find out no blame for what keeps blackness black;
Seek out no causes for th'engender'd lack

Of bite that moves unnurtured souls to track
Corners where edges curve and backtrack back;

Repeat what Repetition overwrites and try
To wring new colours from a sky
Grey and all-rainy in a symmetry
Docked of all ardour, cold and dry;

Do what you can to increase Nature's power;
Grow in old grittiness hour by seething hour;
Pretend pretension shines when sunsets glower
And grin and glisten as the rainstorms shower;

For nobody can do what Nature does:
Take a be-flaken flower imperious
And give it the bone to grow oblivious
Of castigating mockings: 'Be like us!'

To be like, not a flower, but like a tree
That grows, unsapling, finally to be
A goatee'd ape spouting his verses free
Of freedom and of spontaneity,

But filled with casts of vastness and of rhyme
Stomping a rhythm on the face of Time
And jollifying joy as, in his prime,
Did Beethoven, re-Joycing in his theme

Of 'get to Death!' while down the sky
Aeons of starlets roll their stories by
And a limp-like Dawn ends in an Ecstasy
And strident Night becomes a vanquished Eye;

For clarity is for once for aye for all
The rooted heart that breaks the summer's fall

And castigates those leaves that fail to pall
With winds ironic blasting through them all;

Clarity instigates clearness that breaks the fall
From bedded rock to nighttime's gauzing pall,
Upwards a-seeming but downwards pulling all
To where the nighttime greets the summer's fall,

Pulling with urgent feel the taunting pall
That shrouds the shuddering daytime from the all
That brings the sheeted summer and its fall
Onto a leafèd surface where the pall

Of night beshrouds the shuddering earth from all
The symmetries that regulate the fall,
From bloodied good to heaven-scented pall
That saturates and soaks this mindless all.

I

DERIVATION

From what bleak act of thought does art derive?
It seems to saunter from deep hopes that lie
Sequestered in a sojourn till they strive
Upwards, excited, to struggle for the sky.

They meet in mind, but, thwarted by events,
They struggle, concede, resist and strive again.
But darkling in the grey of inner sense,
They cannot be achieved so churn in vain,

Looking for life; but, failing life, they change
To art: images are hopes, colours beliefs,
Lakes and woods replace their inner range,
And graded nights and stars spell inner griefs.

Thus art from thwarted life is forged, and virtue free
Tears from a destitute ambition artistry.

SUBLIMATION

Is poetry a dread disease, a sickness?
Or is it what it claims to be, an art?
Or is all art just sublimation, quickness
Of mind and speech determined by the heart?

One thing is true, that if I had you now
And free were I to stroke your glossy hair
And stroke you, or be stroked by you, a vow
Of silence would fall clamping through the air,

Stultifying talk of how I cried
And glazing tact upon my flood of rhyme
And forcing stationarity on my pen;

For, unresolved, old hopes leap out again
From backgrounds of the mind to cover time
With ceaseless voice one cannot turn aside.

RECONCILIATION

There is no inner hurt that reconciles
A loss that beats unhealed beneath the wings
Of art to a quiet solution: he who sings
Of love too often has escaped its wiles.

And he who never sings is rapt in peace.
Only the fluttering, hurting nightingale
Cries of its inward stars to out-regale
The outward stars with cries of no release.

And the impassioned bard who renders rhymes
Unhaltered to the cries of mob and mass
Knows that his fame can never out-surpass
The simple silence of successful times

When head to head in dark, enclasped embrace
Render to ranting every sonnet's grace.

DECORATION

Where golden boats go gliding by the Sun
And the high ricochet of Moon sails silver by
There will the stars be decorate like none
And Venus, star of all the stars, ride high.

And in that coruscation of the skies
There will my song ride slowly higher and higher;
Before the great begrainedness of the rise
Of all the stars will galaxies sing choir;

And the great Voice that, raging, stilled the seas
Will slowly vanish, usurpate by Love;
And the slow poison of the Rains will cease
With all the antidote that you do prove;

And if this seems just verbiage to your ears,
It doesn't matter: words can give Life to tears.

II

ON HEARING BACH PLAYED ON A GREAT ORGAN

To break the utter sound of fast resuscitation
And endlessly remind, in one swift fugue, of death
That seems inordinate and born of degradation,
Seems the enraptured fate of every organ's breath;

And, whether the sounds re-cannonade through vaulted arches
Or peal aloud in lorn-lit pearls from inner places,
The thorns are always there, as is the thirst that parches,
And every note transcribes another mind that traces,

In sound, the oneness of the now with what was past.
The organ stops. And, mirrored like a vein on peace,
The echo of one's own brain joins on to Bach's at last,
And inner hatreds born of 'God' retract and cease.

On seeing the score of the last song of Schubert's *Winterreise*

You can almost hear the creaking grief,
So subtle is the storm;
Regenerated from belief
That sadness is the norm,
The music picks and frets its way
Over the notes that pianos play.

Locked is the world from outside looking in,
So private is the gloom;
Degenerate from sense of sin
And unrelenting doom,
The music picks and frets its way
Into the keys that pianos play.

Mechanical becomes the mind
That has not yet a true love found.

ON HEARING RICHARD BRADSHAW'S *RING CYCLE*

In Toronto, on September 12–18, 2006, a new opera and ballet house, The Four Seasons Centre for the Performing Arts, had as its inaugural opera performance a complete production of Wagner's cycle of four music-dramas known, in English, as *The Ring of the Nibelung*. Each of the following four poems has as its subject one of the four music-dramas; the German titles can be translated as *The Rhine-gold*, *The Valkyrie*, *Siegfried* and *The Twilight of the Gods* respectively.

DAS RHEINGOLD

> How do I elevate, to pinnacle of Art,
> A dirty dwarf whose urge to grasp and seize
> Sheer Beauty causes her to penetrate
> With laughter every knot-hole in his brain,
> Flinching him up to curse the living world,
> Rendering rogue of him who only yearned
> For what he had not, loveliness of look,
> And turning to scarlet hate what once had been
> Simply inaugural willings named Desire?
> I do so by asserting that the *Ring*
> Begins by showing, as if it were a myth,
> What later would, as legend, reappear
> In *Parsifal*, a replay showing the power
> Of Art to forge a loveliness from Scorn.

DIE WALKÜRE

Fricka wins. The accursèd force uncursed
Of wifely morals *has* to win. No fit or
Other choice exists. Survival wins.
It must. And Music is the ultimate
Survivor because it tells the Truth, and when
Life droneth on in dull, meandering tones,
Throughout the days and unbedraggled nights,
Music attains its nutrients from the heart
And pulls its strength from the long-desiring soul
And peers through the nights to guarantee that rest
Be the one thing *not* attained; Music festoons
Its lurid colours over a wavering sleep
That long ago forgot to dream of dreams
And learned to swaddle days with white banalities.

Siegfried

As of symbolic lust and blood, the red
Of a forest sunset blooms between the trees,
Capturing the cold the night brings back,
Lighting small crevices with upstart flowers.
If only the gasp of capture and the groan
Of death-predation-death had not kept pace
With onward-evolution's stride and step
And predatoriness been rotted from
The growing human brain! But idle hope
It is to hope for hopeless peace in men;
Distraction in love it is must wipe out war;
But the beast is always there, ready to tame
Stupider beasts and frame in horn-calls loud
The predator's prayer that there is no-one cleverer.

GÖTTERDÄMMERUNG

I cannot read the blood-light on the land
As other than lamplit screamings retrograde:
The death of the gods! Nothing to worship! Nada!
No higher power! No deeper calm! Nihil!
And, with the winningest sun-dawn ever staged,
The drama's appalling drama-day is over,
The end of the gods has been at hand and gone.
But the drama was born in an over-accomplished penury,
Forecast by flowers that had no hope of staying
Alive even when laid in a favoured position,
Splayed in a flattened bouquet upon a grave
In a large fat church in a rainy prosperity;
Greatness was forecast by mastering passions;
Greatness arrived when Mammon was added to Bach.

IN MEMORIAM S. GEORGE LAVERTY, MD

Dr. Laverty was well-known in his community for his benevolent approach to his psychiatric patients, many of whom were alcoholics. He was also a prominent painter, some of whose works hang in public places, and a strong supporter of music, particularly that of Mozart. He passed away peacefully in his home on September 7, 2006, aged 83.

> I sat and watched the lush mellifluous chords
> Of Mozart reel and unreel from my hands;
> Steady was silence with its countermands;
> More steady was my thought that had no words;
>
> For music is a golden grain of life
> That spurs encounterings of mind and brains
> With greeted colloquies and soft refrains
> And links our lives, each with its portioned strife,
>
> And causes futures, captured in its sound,
> Solemnly to unreel into directions true
> And steadfast in their questings for the new,
> Yet never veer from solid human ground;
>
> And you, empowering, made the melody
> That scores, and underlines, and moves, this threnody.

III

ON THE FEAR OF GOING MAD

Almighty night crawls at his brain
And through the grilling counter-pain
That wreaks the wrathful symmetry of sight
Into a tardy knowledge of the night
He sees deep madness stalk where once it was before,
The fastnesses of fate relinquish ever more.

Night is intuited, and bereft
Of all that lasting love has left;
The empty searcher seeks and ekes his hours
In empty hostel rooms bereft of flowers
And, dipping into veins of fear and bleakened age,
Pours his embittered hopes into a sonnet's rage;

For all that once was held in him up high as real
Has faded to a dream he saw but could not feel.

PARANOIA

Madness is no mean feat; it spells a loss
That crawls in awful bugbear through the mind;
The inner pain of losing is a cross,
A death incurred because you'd been too kind.
The night that lights in sentinellèd stars
The way from birth to death seems inner Hell;
The sound of children's laughter simply scars
The house of hope one hoped wherein to dwell.
And through the coruscations of the night
Where smiles seem torturous mockings of the true,
No one but you can understand the plight
Of being a you that no one thinks is you.
And so the "I am I" becomes "I'm she or he"
And all the world laughs loud in mockery.

HOSPITAL

The dark night glows across the amber plain
Of the floodlit snow; deep arc-lights clatter
Their veins of light over the white surface;
Blue shadows do not even creep but lie congealed.

That is the fence.

The solemn snow creeps over the quiet field;
Each gust of wind is a frolic of air
As if something would happen to the nothingness;
The stars stand bright like white radios.

These are the grounds.

Red brick means modern, grey means
Dark and old from the receptacle
Of the nineteenth century; men were men
Then, and madmen had no souls.

Those are the buildings.

In the dark night, the wards are hushed;
The lumps of blankets signify sleep;
The odd thump of a card falling
Says that the attendants stay awake.

Let me introduce you.

MADMEN THEN

They put us once in chains and mud;
They said we had no souls;
Though we saw moons and light and dark
They said our minds were holes

Of pit and mire and dark debris,
Scattered, without a brain;
They put us into dungeons deep
And never let us out again.

Our wrists bore marks of fetters raw:
We cried, we are depressed;
They said, no madman has a soul,
So why are you distressed?

They dropped us into water deep:
We cried, we're like to drown;
They said, the mad, they have no soul,
So who are you to frown?

They kept us herded into cells
So small the straw all stank;
They said, the mad, they do not feel
So why stand on your rank?

They sometimes tied us up to stakes;
They said that we were witches,
And as the flames licked round our thighs
They struck with whips and switches;

And all the time our poor dark minds
Asked, who is really mad?

Those whose hearts have given in,
Or those who like being bad?

THE MADMAN NOW

He sat upon a barricaded isle
And watched
The sailing stars climb down the night to die.

He could no longer dream for he had gone
Too far
For one who tried to climb and ride the sky.

And so in cornered dismal, dullened ache
He saw
Nothing but what was inward to the eye.

IV

SACRIFICE

The lamb kicked but did not bleat;
        Its blood
Flowed in channels to the stony ground;
        Its blood
Was nothing save unprincipled present-gift;
        Sacrifice
Lay on the empty altar; God
        Smelt.

The general slept and never smiled;
        Servants
Pottered and crept with wishful empty-steps;
        Servants
Whispered and in his final sleep
        The general
Saw his last battleflag falter and fall
        Underfoot.

Death is gift and death is gold
        Unsavoured;

Alchemy, monopoly, indefatigability
      Unfavoured;
Will and hope and heart and sores
      Unbleeding;
Cartridge of enveloped rose
      Unheeding.

OBLIVION?

If death is oblivion,
The warm nothing I felt in 1492
Or 1066 or 1776 or 4004 BC,
Then I have no fear.

But I have friends
Who fear oblivion more than Hell.
The only way I can understand this
Is to remember a high dive
I once tried:

You sit facing the beach
With the sea's surf below you:
You look up at the sky,
Then topple backwards,
Somersault,
And land feet-first in the ocean.

When I saw the sky
Blue-white with nothing beyond
I knew oblivion
And did not have the courage …
Perhaps the waves had changed
Into rock, and I'd land on my head …

That's why I fear Hell more than oblivion.

BROODING

If I foresaw my death,
Pride would be stronger than fear,
And I would subside
Under the bullet or blast-breath
With unshaken devotion to my brain.

But if death comes suddenly—,
A car crossing a red light,
An octopus, a barracuda—,
Then I shall curse in that thought-blank
Between pain and the long excursion.

But if death should come slowly—,
Cancer, angina, thrombosis—,
I shall spend my time grieving
My moments of unfelt cruelty,
My failure to have conquered religion.

DOVE IN DEATH

Dove in death,
You break on the frail
Palette of your wings
More than song,
And take
On the smooth adornment
Of your cupped head
A sorrowing breath

Unscathed because you do not know
The nature of your broken wing
And cannot uphold
On the blood of your beak
That darkens your feathers
The exorbitant
Demands of a dawn
Where no winds blow.

DEATH-IN-LIFE

I held a row of death's blown-open stones
And from their granite fashioned empty bones
And when I sought for flesh to bring them birth
I found no stronger breath than that of earth.

I opened up a coffin full of dreams
And hung their shells on strange and empty streams
And as the waters shook the falling leaves
I found no further rhyme than that of 'grieves'.

18TH-CENTURY DEATH

After the doctors bled him
He lay surrounded by wood
And sighing saw the window
Filled with a sky of glittering grey;

Like balsam on his sickness
Its light arrayed his bedclothes
Till he heard the doctors coming
Climbing up the creaking stairs.

The door opened, the sky seemed
To grow into a darker grisaille,
The doctors entered and fussed
With watches and things of iron;

And as his blood left him
He sank with a hope back
To his pillow that grey, nun's
Hors d'oeuvre, would envelop

His final posing thoughts. Be they
Spiritual, he hoped, as pain
Crept from his chest and clutched
With hands his grey and aching brain.

THINKING

The lonely days when the wind
Brings the uplilted wavetops awash
And cascades leaves over the streets

Seem to augur lonelier days;
Will I fill my age with nothing,
Refreshed because I am not forced

To think, persuaded by casualties
Of indifference and overtones of uselessness?
Or will the wind speak

Of quieter deaths, the peace of spring,
With every squirrel a jot of life
On the page of the opening daffodils?

Age seems something to prepare for,
But the nastiest thing I ever heard
Was somebody saying they had children

In order to have friends in oldness.
I think few poets love life;
There is too much meanness in it.

And the most sensible statement
Seems to be by a French *madame*
Who said, 'to have children

Is the cruellest thing one can do'.
Wind, blow the waves higher,
And let your anger keep me alive:

The secret of death is independence,
The secret of age is emotion,
And the secret of life is creation.

THE ATHEIST'S DEATH

When bone meets bone
Nobody stands:
We fall alone.

And into night
Our blood-red fall
Carries a song

Like a madrigal;
Its open heart
Fails, furious fast,

And onto death
We fall
At last.

Our regal minds
Swift in endeavour
Falter and pale;

Along the sea
A lone man sings
A whisper-thrall;

A seagull wings
Up from the waves
Harrying;

The tiny sands
Knock like nerves
On frozen hands.

Hard and unkempt
Like a tree
In a storm

Our ghosts and fancies
Take on
Hollow form;

And as the sea
Waves falteringly
Across the bay

We light a candle
Making night
A lovesick day.

Formerly once,
Modernly twice,
Future-wise thrice

The gates entice
The lonely soul
To freeze on ice

And watch for eyes
That crawl in space,
A carapace

Hard and enduring
Over the stars
Never alluring.

And as the chill
Creeps up until
The nerve-cells fade,

We see the dark
Upheld, embark
On prowless boats

Over a sea
Of foam and phlegm,
The apothegm

Of boldly going,
Sighing and soughing,
The physic arc.

And all the end
Can hold
Is foe or friend,

Empty reactions,
To old
Interactions,

And last of all
We ask, who said
The most

We hold in this
Our final bed:
The serpent's hiss.

Purgatory

Purgatory calls a rye-dale soft
Nothing of asphodel meadows, nor naught
Of lava and smoky caves
Encounter the broad and lofty
Skies that silver-wail arch
The softer pools and valleys.

Across the fields, I see old friends;
We smile and talk of enemies,
Delilahs, Caligulas, Attilas;
A frozen army of Romans stands
Like stones at the head of the valley.

There are thunderstorms here and lightning
And lions and poison ivy and locusts;
Under the windswept peak of the night
Cicadas shrill and somehow the air
Is a darkened tangle of polar and tropical.

Purgatory is the same as Earth,
Where we're damned for doubting,
Disliked for fighting, despised for suffering,
Praised for succeeding, dampened for laughing
And kicked for preferring truth to beauty.

STEALTH

When under veils of smoky death
Blue rainbows curve and part the sky,
The overladen rage of breath
Bursts out in stealth
And blows the land and deserts dry;

And into night our bodies roll,
Stealing a doldrum from the moon
Until a fear strikes from each pole
And climbs the blackness till
The earth is swathed in damask gloom.

STANDING AND WATCHING

I cannot halt what craves to be halted,
Growing in soft equations overnight
To the grim enunciation of endness;

And so I stand and watch, slightly aghast,
As the humming orbits of my cells
Tinker with halting fastness the peripheries,

Ends, junctions, transpositions, crenellations;
Soft as the simple web of blood blooming
Stands like a prayer my grey, collapsèd self.

GRAVESTONES

Inglewood and Overton, names like Archigrade,
Names, names, names ...
    How still the gravestones are
    In comparison with the movement underneath!

Lie in cold corruption, store the ancient core
Of heart solid as dust ...
    How still the yew tree is
    In comparison with the beetles inside it!

Take unwearied eyes, and fractionate each orbit
Into unpleasant lacerations ...
    How still the church strives high
    In comparison with the bowed-down worshippers!

Thus the untaken, unmoven, unbroken till light
Is gone into putrescent darkness ...
    Thus the organic in nerve-strung
    Harmony with the movement of sodden earth.

VISTAS

I stood on a high forsaken rock,
My back to rock, my eye to valley;
Green as a river streamed the fields,
With pine-trees the cloaking of riverside banks;
I stood and I smelt no death.

I stood by a stream, and the ripples
Tensed each water-pulse as if to pull
The enshrouding higher and further; the faster,
The inner; time tinkled; bubbles quivered;
I stood and I smelt no death.

I stood in a square by a market-tent,
Counting the apples and hearing coins clink;
Somebody threw a pale red awning
Over a countertop; raindrops tickled;
I stood and I smelt red death.

WORDINESS

Arguments flow like cinders from crucibles,
Open air dilettantes flaunt, like flat wands,
Rhetoric concerning death and life, Roman
Pillars stare, Gothic arches shrug, Palladian
Mansions shiver, Baroque churches slumber.

So many words about death and hope
Have floated ever longingly like bells
Over the sober lancets of hall and manse
That the exorbitant hills fall short
In their breathing; the meadows slumber.

And the fortune-tellers and the astrologers
Maintain with a long strong arm of fortitude
That life is theirs, that like clouds they forecast
The onset and encumbrance of doom, the end
Of the questioning eye that stares at theirs.

And Death all the time hides himself
Under shrubs, under bushes, ascertaining
The whens and whys of deceasement:
Only the cells too small to see, or theorems
About force and mass, contain the responses.

QUIET LIGHT

Quiet light held in a solemn bed the air of nights:
The stars made white the desert, sand seemed snow,
The gusting of dunes against the rocks made frozen shade.

CASKET

The corpse is loaded down with artefact
And the utter stillness robs the air of breath;
The elders stand and mutter words of tact
While teenaged daughters think of their own death.

Then, when death's silence seems more still than dead
And the quiet white head that once aloud did breathe
Lies in a casket flowered with white and red
Around which drapes of damask flow and wreathe,

Then, in that silence broken by dull talk
The solitary corpse knows nothing of their grief,
Or of the carelessness the atheists hawk
Who have no fear of death with their belief;

The atheists look while priests intone and bless:
Atheists have no questions in their earthliness.

RETROSPECT

And, like so many aged and aching men,
I scan the far horizons of my past,
Seeing lost oceans lost in spans of time
And waiting for a sun to shine at last;

And dark hale wholes of lifetimes overcome
Penetrate hard the present's aching while;
Rainbows seem lostness redolent of youth
And inner starshine seems to stop and smile

Till Now sequestered is by veils of sleep
And all the oceans fade and cross the sea
To a low calm hummock of benevolence
That seems to mock the hopes that used to be;

And into sleep rock latitude and quiet demise
As lasting sleep blocks deathlike the veil of inner eyes.

WHY?

And when I see, in thick-profoundèd death,
All that is gold turn thick to muddied mire,
And know that what I see is never really there,
But only lingers mentally like a breath,

Then are pure words pure fault of reasoning;
They search for meaning, solid referent;
Only the pointer points, emollient;
No object ends his reconnoitring.

What does he look for, clad in his poet's stance?
Why is his knowledge stippled upon his cloak?
Why does he monitor his every dream that broke
And list in a file his follies of romance?

Because he does not care to remonstrate
Against a god who changed His name to 'Fate'.

Fear

I could not look on Death, which, being unknown,
Dealt me the fear I only knew once before,
When I tried to dive backwards from a board
On to a rocky Mediterranean tidewater.

Then I saw nothing but whiteness, for the sky was white;
Death showed me nothing but darkness; but the sky
Should have been blue, and, as for Death,
Well, I can't have known it for I'm still here.

And when demons of my childhood scream from Hell,
Or I dream of my green-eyed Beatrice in Heaven,
I know that my fear of Death is not of the unknown,
But that I might survive and find that I was wrong.

V

CHILD AWAKENS

The golden, half blue-white of dawn
Etches its palette
Across the corners of your room
In a dulcet silhouette;

Into the edges of your room
The cat pads, slinting-eyed;
You turn, half breathe, half wave, half cross
An arm across your side;

And in some ochre dream, you turn;
Daylight evokes a half-cry;
And into a half-dawn would you wake
Without a lullaby.

CHILD AT PLAY I

On the ground your feet touch stones
As your eyes search for treasure;
Each glint of mica is gold,
A fallen coin a link of Zeus's chain.

In the air your hair is golden
As your ears listen for cuckoos;
Each hiss of leaf-wind bustle
Is a broken string of Aeolia's lyre.

In the breeze your body battles
Innocently against the world's forces;
Its unconsciousness is its beauty;
It never tries to be spontaneous.

Art is the manufacture of intellect,
Its subject matter, artlessness.

CHILD AT PLAY II

The rings the sun forms on the rings
                Of circled hair
Are antidote to crippled kings,
Unsightly queens, offensive things
To which all children silent witness bear;

And in their limelight laughter palls
                The dew of rain
From tears and blows and hazard falls,
Accidents and scrapes and brawls,
And children's ventures that subside in pain;

Thus is the black on the silver white
                Their eyes reflect:
Concoctions from a never-ending night
Of underspoken suffering and blight
From which a child's ambitions resurrect.

Child at Play III

Although your eyes are pearled with nascent lustre
And the long clean strop of your flesh is pure,
So that you walk with a step that's firm and sure,

The novelty of the shadow that your hair makes
Against the enormous aura of the autumn sky
Has the quiet resonance of hopes that cannot die;

But I see your hopes as illusion, can scarcely bear
To watch you smile and scuff against each leaf;
Hope is an arcady treasure that rusts to disbelief.

CHILD AT NIGHT

With no fear, the echo of shafts of starlight
Strikes like sound on the heart of midnight;
Walk, let shadows girdle your hardness,
Your hardness of ego in frail innocence.

Each underfoot grass-blade strikes like a flail
Backwards ready for dew and for loss;
Each step is a glance of your innocent eyes;
Each step is assertion of your strong childhood.

Under the branches of moon-dusted beeches
The sigh of your breathing is halt, fast, shrill;
Your breath is engenderment of wilfulness,
The night a shroud of vagueness and dark.

If I have seen you before, it is I
Who, half-seen, saw my self in shroud
And perspective of echoed potential;
The night is not your cape, but your sleep.

CHILD ASLEEP

Though empty lies the dream beyond the curtain,
Beyond the toys to what you see, the world,
Sleep holds in haltered hands the last of Nighthood
And openings and startings lie unfurled.

Though sleep can stop and the dreamer wake,
Though night can wait and the daylight bold
Open with shaking hands the mind's carnation
And in it dreams of Nighthood faint unfold.

These are the dreams of mine: they are not yours.
Your head is lost in silence and in grey,
So that the head I see as yours is my head
And all the Nights that crowd it, Selfhood's day.

VI

THE NERVES

The nerves know their way:
They saunter or jump like climbing vines,
Seeking the sunshine of flesh,
Arterial management, ensconcement of limb;

The brain knows its way:
It points out its convoluted eye,
The cells burn like pinpricks
On their white honeycomb;

The heart has its say:
Like a knock-burst it speaks
First to the growth of the inborn
Then to the flux of its maker;

The skull has its say:
Like a coordinate shell-bomb
Slowly it will slide
To be first to feel day.

THE VEINS

Until the wide hill-path
Of upward climb of veins,
Arteries, lymph-canals, nerves
Arrives at the head, the heart,
Encumbered with nothing but blood,
Forces instilled *Über*-flowers
Of pulses and energized upbeat
To fill the nodular spaces.

The growing eye, the outgrowth
Of ear, the small stencil of fingers,
Toes in extortionate raiment,
All adhere to the minuscule;
Growing in flood, the placenta,
Feeding and nurturing slowly,
Absorbs and assists the enhancement,
All in a molecule moment.

THE STORM

Outside, the storm held handfuls of light,
Tumblings of air, ricochets of sound;
Inside, the oval awning of protection
Held you in silence, hardly breathing.

Outside, the sun span sunwebs of sheer heat;
The sky lay in drunken ochre to the north;
Inside, your half-formed veins and arteries
Carried the heat and kept you cool and warm.

Outside, the night lay dank like orchid layers,
Flowers the stars, the stems arched nightlight frondings;
Inside, your eyes were closed and night
Held you in heartbeat arms in arc umbilical.

ALONE

Arcane in solitude,
Its only new knowledge
Fingernails and hairs,

The foetus opens
A cornered eye
And sees dark.

One cell too many,
One gene too much,
One over-surfeit

And the foetus
Closes its heart,
Loses its spark.

VII

NIGHT-THOUGHT

Encouraged by the quietness of the twilight,
The verdant trees spread their silver-dappled leaves
To the slow red of the sunset. Eager-horned,
A crescent moon seems caught like a sliver
In a web of furry cloud. The quiet countryside
Seems caught in two motions, one flat, seen from the air,
The other smooth and sliding as from a train.
The two revolve and coalesce, and the night
Sears its enormous burden down in a brown cover-all;
The air is quiet and submits and all is peace.

Motion evolving is movement, but moonlight is
Motion evolving as mood. Light is a sharp and crescendo,
The dark the incorporate blue. Black is a force
And escape hatch, the light that evolves into force.
Colour is crescent candescent, the ache of the making
Is new. The ache of the making is you. The
Night bleaks a new night right-making.
The arch of the sky is askew.

The night is a light-lying vapour.
The light is inviolate too.

ILLICIT LOVE

Locked in one doleful whole through wholesome lust
The cursèd pair stands, lost in each other's eyes,
While sunset pours its radiance like trust
To thwart each person's mind from compromise.

Stand locked, entrusting lovers, do not yield,
Though the high sky boil over into fire;
What you possess stands unrepressed, so shield
Your inner trust with even more desire.

For though the skies boil, and the raging firmament
Cries with a god-like anger that you sin,
What you possess stands stressed as armament
To steel your souls till one day you may win.

And when the day comes that you may ease your hold,
The steel that grasps you tight will turn to gold.

EPITHALAMION

When in broad shadows walks the stealth of night
Then are you not alone; he who abides
Has in his strong encountered hands beholden
You to his day; night no more walks but glides
Past in a glimmer, glazed with a softened lore.

Do not encounter petulance with petulance, take
In a sort of savour each enchanted day
Till a great still dawn of evenness suffuses
The two-to-onenesses; days no more pass, but stay
Alert to newnesses and novelties to store,

For in a fusion fickle flares black night
To gaze in fawning golden on his prey:
Only a far-flung bodylock of minds
Will keep a wedlock longer than a day.

Museum Piece

A female beauty in a vial of Time:
Observe the resplendent relic cast in rhyme
That wears each moment's magic like a rune
Magic in rhythm, more magic still in tune;

Observe the quiet rapt blush upon each cheek,
Faintly obsessed with looking not too meek
And yet not anxious to be full of character
For only mildly mad folks play the actor;

And see the hair down-falling to the back,
Gently a-sway and swaying, smooth and slack,
Unhampered by barrettes, not braided tight,
A hair to handle, loose and lax and light;

And see the lips that only kissed a child,
Faintly obsessed with looking not too mild,
That hail a gold *carrosse* with silver words
That wing across the air like silken birds;

And see the glowing fullness of the thighs
Swaying to svelte the swelling upward rise
Of haunch attached and narrowing to the waist
That no desirous hand has yet embraced.

See, see this female beauty in her vial:
Look at it now and ponder if this style
Of picturing her is old and dead and dry,
And, if you think it is, please tell me why.

TRUTH

Dress thy lovely neck with ropes of pearl—
But do not hide the folds
That grew from statured bending
Of the head thy neck upholds.

For structure functions carefully,
Nature it designs:
Dress thy lovely neck with ropes of pearl—
But do not hide its lines.

Knight

A knight: the concept is dead,
Like a wreath of water-wrack
On a golden grave.

Everything is practical now. When
A knight's head rears to catch
A glint of oceanic spear
On his helmet, he is mocked.

And should a poet veer in verse
Knight-like to approach the goal
Of errant rivalries and poise
His steel unrendered in frail
Agonies of light, he is rejected.

DESIRE POEM

Engines of arcanity bewilder and pulse
My forlorn and totally lost muse-machine.
You see, I think in circles, symbols,
Fugues, chords, all nicely wrapped, pocketed
With injections of symbol-causes, the antique
And the coruscate modern bedeck
The Léger-like sides of white and metal
Curves, pounding, thumping *machinery*;

But the very whisper, the very flutter
Of your white hand on me, the movement
Of a silent smile of expectation—wait—
Reaching—nearly: oh, the control
Of you, tendering your mental fingers
Against the pocketings, the ratchetings,
The gears, the worms, the screw-threads,
The silent monotonous pulse-moves;
The machinery is gone, it *melts*;

And so like a quiet clock turning over
In its sleep, sullenly muffling chimes,
Bellows gone wrong, subsided in breath,
My brain-machine sighs, shudders, moans,
Cries "Make me two, not one", sobs,
Sees crescent-like an opalescent tear
On the pillow; and, totally unmechanically,
A soft white fever of challenge calls
The softness to grow velvet-hard and ape
The new softness of music in *your* mind.

Form

If I bring in form,
Fractionate into distillates prosody,
Alembic the aleatory,
My brain is running away from you.

Is that a comfortable land
That encapsulates the cerebral,
Inaugurates an initiative?
Without you, hollow and empty.

My land is merging
Mellowing monsoons and tarnish
Vanishing into evanescence,
No, *e*merging.

O THOU

O thou in a soft mourning,

Gaze on me, you other, let me shade and raise my hand
Against the total unrecalcitrance, the orb-shining of your blue
  gaze.

O thou in a soft mourning,

I stand entranced, the golden of each fine and rapid notion
Of your hair is like the weaving of a siren's song of gold.

O thou in a soft mourning,

Harps from your hair, clarions from your eyes, trumpets
From the unveiled movement of the avenging beauty of you!

O thou in a soft mourning,

Oh why, when the sunshine captures me, pulls me out,
Reaches into my deepest chord of heart, must there be weeping?

O thou in a soft morning,

There must be none. The sunshine must be silent. A
Crystalline firmament has to encase our sun-world. O

THEME

By a gentle sort of crime, her mind would,
He felt persuaded, come to appreciate him more
For his soft affection and gentle stream of good.
But her hands fell on a harder man who bore
The burden of her love more lightly than he ever could.

He watched them walk, enveloped mind to mind,
While his empty hands seemed trapped in webs of wood.
Only a subtle difference of the place and kind
Had hindered him from doing what he knew he should.
But now he stood, to dull defeat resigned,

Seeing with sullen insight what he'd lost.
As only the loser knows to count the cost,
So only the loser knows the fiercer thrust
That loss of love is worse than loss of lust.

VARIATION I

The golden light that claims the Arno river
And shields it with upholden golden skies
Declaims the virtues of the witless giver
While he who holds back giving claims the prize.

The artist fiercely claims a Giotto grotto,
The poet faint from passion heavy sighs,
And while the world proclaims their every motto
The man who's free from passion claims the prize.

The soft and gentle hide and claim compassion,
The ardent swain cows Hades with his cries,
But while a kind gentility's the fashion,
It's inner force that wins the fairest prize.

Do not go gentle therefore into Eros' fray:
Only the strong and selfish win the day.

VARIATION II

To wallow in self-pity is an organ-grinder's task;
You turn the wheel, the wails come out
And friends like monkeys churn about
Wondering what they dare and dare not ask;

But truth it is you do not dare to eye;
You do not dare to face your inner soul,
Its weakness is so weak you lose your goal
And sink suffusing in a bath of 'Why?'

For truth it is that brings about resent,
For truth tells true that all you want is love
From someone stronger, grander, more above
Self-pity than yourself, magniloquent;

But if you meet her, watch your wooing well:
A rival suit will bring a rival hell.

VARIATION III

The end of the game is when she holds his hand
Unconsciously, an instinct he reciprocates.
Then you treat friends and strangers like subordinates
And feel so hurt you find it hard to stand.

This is true love, and often comes too late.
All mad philosophies and crude religions fade
Into a jostle of empty shapes in shade
Before the strength of love you cannot hate.

She walks beside you but she is not yours.
To see her happy pains your aching heart.
That happiness should be from you, and art
Is a straitened comfort that only rarely cures.

Time, they all say, will make it go away.
But so much time will pass that you'll be grey.

Variation IV

No light can penetrate the sense of dark
In one who's seen his deepest dream dissolve;
Only the hope of newness hardens his resolve
To get to death unshackled by his madness,
To get to death undriven mad by sadness.

And in the world on which he hopes to lay his mark
Round him lie loves unfettered by deception;
Dreamer and dream are fused in clean conception,
Smilers lie smiling, untrammeled by confusion,
Skies smile with sunshine, blooms glow in profusion.

But life to him seems dark and dullen dour,
Time seems to creep in minutes through each hour,
And every day conceals a bitter cross
And every night a solitude and loss.

I DO NOT LIKE YOU, BUT I ...

As the side of your face
Laid its lovely curve
Against the air that slid
À côté of it

I conjectured with a halting,
A sort of mind-murmur,
A kind of solid heart-stop,
That your beauty

Was something I invented.
And then I knew I lied
For out of my eye's corner
I saw your ankle.

What, an ankle? What is this,
A Victorian joke? No,
Your ankle laid its lovely curve
Against the air that slid
At its side in perfection;

And my head then stopped
Its broadly rolling course;
My thought stopped in
A kind of fear;
Was I up to it?
Could my words do it?
Could they render your perfection
From the closet of now
To dizzying space
Of the future? But it

Was a moment's halt
Not a burst I am writing about
And at that halt
I felt all chiding childlike
Leave the loping leap
Of my moral me
And stop in a sort of ecstasy.

I DO NOT LIKE YOU, BUT …

You spin my thundered words again, like a Fate.

Whether you stand alone, or are shadowed by dual thees,
The endless hum of your spinning-wheel strikes the clouds

That gather in furling furrows about you with sound.
It penetrates them; but in their refulgence it spreads like colours
From sunlight refracted through glass, and grows chords;

And they spin from where you are, where you are sitting,
In silence, evading the sunlight, and stride
Over the distant spaces of winter to me like inordinate orders.

My brain is white, splintered, broken into its furrowed anatomy
By the breaking of time's white waves upon its lobes;
But the corded knots still hold, they are undestroyed
By the ravages of my broken lust for you and my greyed
And tarnished hope; and what chords you play, unfettered

By the unison of the single tone of the spun web's play,
Reach and touch into those bright white neurones that spread
Like threads, awaiting the music's touch; they are frightened to
    life;
They awaken, take on colours, erect from spun to woven,
Jangle like broken harps being joined together rapidly,

So rapidly, it is a Heaven's hands which join them, and they fit.
From space, all-space too equated for equations, they rouse sound.
And yours are the hands which, broken by veins, hardened
By nails, lined from work, coiled and recoiled by fingerprints,
Start them to sound. A single line of spun thread rhymes

Through the clouds and awakens the carpet of my nerves' harps.
I waken and watch you, in silence, spin the spun fate of my song.

I DO NOT LIKE YOU …

Wild and grey to Boscombe made there I
Love's decision;
Over, planed a sea-skirt nacre sky
Of sky's precision;
Beneath, laved waves of welter-water sea
Within the rock's incision;
The sea and sky poured console over me,
And love, derision.

I DO NOT LIKE …

Arcadian reeds may quiver in the wind
And summer's light bedeck Orcadian isles
But you, in winter-dress, stand open-skinned
And wreck my high-flung whimsies with your smiles.

And when, if I should wander off in doubt
To scatter scattered oddments of my art
On verses parched from intellectual drought,
You firmly stand and firmly play your part.

You do not act, but stand there firm-in-flesh
Always gold-solid, enhardened in reality,
Ready to catch my whim-thoughts in your mesh
And melt them into merciless banality.

I DO NOT LIKE THIS ...

What if black jealousy's augured robe
Denoted loss? Would the anger suffice
To kill the loss, or would it suffuse
To tears, each drowning in momentary loss
The awful aggravation of the anger?
Jealousy looks like bleakness, but is black;
No higher anger fills the head, nor
Can humiliation on political grounds
Aggrieve like the loss of a love, a paramour.
I waited, could not stand the psychic smell
Of half-intentions, semi-formulations,
Half-hinged-out desires while nearness,
Not of soul or brain, but of interests
Drew you together, spiking a spear
Into the half-swelled blood of my brain.
Then, no inoculations of apology, medications
Of regret, or indignations at my jealousy
Suffice to fuse the whole to negation;
I *am* jealous, and these darkening lines
Are testament to the dolour of my jealousy.

... BUT *THEY* DO ...

They meet when daylight draws the moon
Down to a bed to meet the sun;
They meet when night grows stars like flowers
That wilt to prove when night is done;
They meet when the sea grows golden flames
And all its waves are fused as one.

VIII

Seasons

Wrench a tear from every leaf, or else a bubbled flower
Smelling of the high green
Of the overvalent larches, sprigs and buds of lower spruce;

For dark green hides the winter, and light green spears the spring,
And into the wide bowl of the lake
The marbled drops of fall are like red stars strewn in glass.

Craven seem the shoots as the April cloud darkens the light
And the sun stands like a eunuch
Holding a pale grey veil over his body which has no gleam;

But when a current of eddying air from the North or South
Breathes away the cloud like a mile-
Width feather the leaves sigh from moulded red to sage

And then to yellow-green, quiet sunshade of the yellow sun,
Dappled with spheres of silver as the rain
Falls like a spraywain, chariots dragging the day.

So summer adds her flatter viridian, heat glazes over
The initial ripeness, and the older trees
Armoured with empty branches are like crotchets on the black

And white of the form of a coloured fugue; and fall
Steals in like an old man with empty bottles
Who upends each over each leaf and drags them into gold;

And the winter starkens the window-scene, creases
Each fold with icicle lancets
And memories clothe each bony branch with livingness.

Wrench a tear from every leaf, or else a bubbled flower
Smelling of the high green
Or the overvalent larches, sprigs and buds of lower spruce.

Spring I

A raven on the glacial bank
Is life in black on broken white;
The ice floats barque-like on the lake
And sunlight strikes its flanks with light;

Like light, a solemn crow cries 'craak',
Evens the flow of the lake's blue cold,
And over a misty island's back
Rivers of sky show streaks of gold.

Will the moon bring more of ice, or break
Into fine sunlight flaked with breeze?
A silhouette of a flight-winged rook
Cries of a nest in the brown-tipped trees.

SPRING II

The eye turns in its orbit
                overwhelmed
By the tininess of colour
                of a crocus bedded
In soil that knew the burden of snow.

The cry of a bird reminds
                the blustery air
Of the emptiness of winter's birdsong;
                along
The road the grass is uncrushed
                and green
Where snow had burned
                it brown.

In winter a house's stone grey
                sang like a photograph
Of an old leaden song; its white
                is now song-thrush
White as the sun slides against
                its new splendour.

The eye turns back and in itself
                knows renewal;
The tattered cobwebs of inturned
                winter-nothing
Unfold and embed bright visions
                that see spring
On the bordered crosswork of revival.

AUTUMN

Now autumn brings her slow, sad-veiling light
Upon the upholden barren; the grass grows dull,
No trees are here to sparkle the air
With their red dust and yellow sheen and gold;

But in the forest, all is lightened, cusping
The sky with new blue, the rivulets with rushed white;
The brown of the earth is darker and the songs
Of the departing birds louder over the gone green.

Dawn

The border of a misty land
Hangs, fog-like, in the shroud
Of the mist; the ship heaves
On the slow lassitude of the wave.
Night's dark has gone, morning
Is white, silent the seagulls.
The cliff sighs in the mist
As the low lapping of water
Signals ship-arrival in harbour,
With the land's misty borders
Hanging fog-like off the prow.

The sky is gone, lost in mist;
The sail hangs, flaps quietly,
A murmur of canvas on the great
Painting of the white dew-laden
Morning: override of grey, sigh
Of white, as the morning's
Mists unmask the misty borders
Of the land. The fog hangs
Thick, the timbers creak, and
The low-lying blink of the port's
Lights, two or three, beckon
The ship into harbour.

Morning

I felt the solemn morning all in air
And the first clock struck
With chimes that wandered clear

Across the horizon from the sheet
Of dawn spreading in awesome light
To the last star of the dark.

Nobody shelved an oar, yet the splashes
Were so dim-dullened by the sound
Of the clock, that the men stopped

Incipiently to count the hours to day
On the notches of their knuckles, and watched
The droplets melt away in the sun's haze.

DAYTIME

Listen where the frail whispers of the grasses in the marshes
Light like a shell on the plain of the open waters;
Listen where in the still of the noon the corn is silent
And its sentinels stand like a mask to enliven the heat;
Listen when in the falling dusk a redwing lights
On a fence and stands like a shadow conducting the evening;
Listen, for over all these refinements of the day
Cloud-Pan blows his pipe with its notes as a robe for events.

NIGHTTIME

When evening songs spin star-spun webs from night
And the lone murmurs fall of birds' half-drowsing sleep
And the black lattice of branches fades into more moonlit grey,

The loneliness of the unwatched lover sigh-asserts itself,
The weeds are black, dust and dirt-ridden bricks lie in the grass,
The hostility of rust smuttens the even smoothness of the
    grass-blade,

The moonlight is anchored to girders of ancient humiliations.
The bats frisk and push their echoes over unseeing veins of brain,
The night takes on a stench and an odour of 'why me?',

But in the cool and quite unhostile layers of the dawn,
As the eastern sky begins to elevate itself in a layer of white grey,
The greying moon and the greying mists at the edge of the lake

Take on auroric gleams, spiders' webs are minuscule pearl-strings,
And a stalwart rage sends 'Past' into oblivion, and Future begins.

IX

STILL LIFE BY CÉZANNE

Why, in the golden slumber of nectarines,
The intangibility of blue should
Seem enconched like a dark shell
In the sloping lap of an ocean

Is the 'why'; and the like-molluscs
Of each tasseled brush-stroke, hard
But infiltrated with the softness of
Glowing fruit caught in a final tessella
Of sunset, have each their single reply.

Departure from Cythera by Lorrain

Embroidered and bordered by the fall
Of a fine sun-sweep so that the light
Wraps in green dusk the falling portraits
Of windows, ruins, antique foliage,

The light falls and catches in a glimmer
Of halo superiorities of helmets
That glimmer like golden dusk
On spearpoints and highlights
The grief of women watching soldier-boats depart.

A Chair by Van Gogh

Worn and unwelcome, the chair
Is sitting slowly and alone, as if
To move were burthen of Sisyphus
Rolling sunlight up a slope

Made of cracked attic-wood; yet
The chair has corners, back and legs
And thus is ready (if only ready!)
For to be moved or picked up—
Or maybe dusted so that admiration emerge?

A Soldier by Rembrandt

Here peers somebody, somebody, somebody
Standing in half-pride at the respect
His own and coward darkness fill
Him with, so being born that way;

And stands there, he is somebody,
Stands there, look at somebody,
Somebody, somebody, why light
Has even bounced off me! Look,
I have no drum, I am all ears.

A Girl On A Swing by Fragonard

Hurtle up, flowers, all white and dew
As up she swings into the trees:
Up that you catch what will be, what will be,
And the flowers of earth be made flowers on a tree!

Look, flowers, look, she stops!
Her hand in a curtain of Nature gropes,
As balànces she, as balànces she,
And starts on the downward swing
Ready for more, as she scrapes by your tingling petals!

WORK BY HOLMAN HUNT

O violent Work, which sobers all our days
And brings coherence to time, and robs
All of us from concentration on the heart
That it not break, like dirty iron in rain,

Teach us to worship our raw-baked hands
Whose veins are like scaffolding over the sun,
Whose palms are like heartbeats in dull cafés,
Whose nails are pink as bills and forms,
Whose futures are hardened by what must be done.

Water Lilies by Monet

It is their encouraging size which we love,
These sloping and floating embroachments of nenuphars,
Floating in openness over green water that curls
In lovely softened washes, that ripples

In thirsty drops, that splashes your whiteness.
It is their encouraging size which we love—
Are all flowers so open? Art thou open?
Can I compare thee to a summer's day?
Art thou a flower? Art thou?

Dancing Girls by Matisse

All in a brown and ochre afternoon …
Or is it the red that sings of
Blood they exemplify, the twitching dancing forms
Holding hands in each hand, all joined

By everted virtuosities of joints?—They dance,
The enfolded cumbersomenesses of weight
Of colour join in the dance—They dance
The cardinal light of colour companions
Their dance, they dance, in redness.

An Op Art painting by Vasarely

Kaleidoscoping through an oval called
Kaleidoscope which is not just a line
Quick-formed and staggered through a failing
Look that glances at the quickprint of the

Stereoscope that forms a blinkered glass
Over the ovally ovary of perception.
That is the quick glance of the silver light
Your pointed pencil pierces in perception
And rounds off to a perfect O of ignorance.

X

Rainbow

A rainbow running down from sky
That brought bright light-flash raindrops by
Took blueness from an overcloud
And laid it lake-down like a shroud.

No weather's wane or thunder-crash
Can chase away a raindrop's flash,
For every atom-smite lays down
A rim of droplets like a crown

And thus is nought but certitude
That all that happens, happens crude:
A blunder forms from a slight aside,
A chronicle from an artist's pride,

A cataract from a fall of hail,
A star-fall from a comet's tail,
A mountain from a mound of dust,
And a poem from a pang of lust.

RHETORIC

Although I give a rhetoric of love
Which, did I not love, I never could,
Remember this, in cold and solemn thought:
Poetry is a portrait of the blood.

And when it's hot and my eyes grow fire
And you're there, the words are flames;
But all I can do if you play with me
Is pout and call you names.

For poetry is the child of fire,
The fusion of love and lust;
To cheapen it to insult
Is to douse the fire with dust.

INSPIRATION I

I cannot carve your winsome powers
Or strike in sombre aptitude the questionings
And intriguings that enrobe your hours;

But in a moment's rage of inward quest
I struck your eyes askance, and watched in dance
The overplay of raining stars that dressed

The sky with a quiet overplay of light,
A light that struck in a green ray from your eyes
And robed in a remnant redolence the night.

So at a moment's force the verses came:
I stopped at a pillar's grey to write them down;
I cannot force apology or take the blame

For wishing to enhance a fabled gaze
With an undoubting poem in your praise.

INSPIRATION II

No matter how we phone or write
Or speak, no matter what we say,
The next few days are full of verse
From which I cannot keep away

And everything I see or hear
Or smell or touch or taste
Becomes a symbol linked with you,
Not one of which I waste:

The lake becomes great Nature-you,
My chairs become your bed,
My books become your intellect,
My hands become your head,

Even the empty morning light
Becomes your sleeping whole;
The only thing I haven't found
Is a symbol for your soul.

INVOCATION

O thou who sleeps where the dark streams mill
And agitatest the waters with thy hands,
Anchoring rocks to screes that roll the folding hill
Into communion with the river's strands,

Stand fast and firm upon thy leaman's staff
And do not more in cogitating rue;
Stand where thou werst, still like a photograph:
Never undo what thou wast proud to do.

For in thy heart and in thine eyes' domain
Solemn security stands like a golden door;
Where the crowd's weakness pulls me down again,
Thou standest firm, a fixèd paramour;

And if I'm ever asked if name thou hast,
'Muse' I shall say and stare at thee aghast.

WHITE GODDESS

They brought me through to where the day,
Rayoned and stagèd in laced gold,
Ate the horizon; and there by a finely fretted poplar
They prepared a bier of thistles and tall ferns and marigolds
And laid me upon it; but a Moon no one had noticed
Drew fearlessly from a scabbard of stars a hook like a hawser
And threw it to me and bade me climb to her.

In the Mists

In the mists of ardent time
The lines of furrowed forests climb
The slopes of castled mountains formed
Of story saga song and rhyme

And, in the golden light that shines
From suns that swim in brimming lines
From rim to rim of bordered sky,
Time telescopes, and life entwines,

And all comes focussed, flash and fore:
The elegant, the carnivore,
The light, the lash, the plague, the feast,
The rogue, the saint, the manticore.

978-0-595-45577-5
0-595-45577-8

Printed in the United States
98845LV00003B/151-249/A